Foreword

"Many children anticipate and even long for a summer vacation to an exciting destination that they have never visited. This book takes children on a journey across Mississippi, while addressing still-too-common misconceptions about the state in an age-appropriate manner. This book entertains the reader while showing that Mississippi is a wonderful state with wonderful people. I believe this book will instill pride in Mississippi's children, as well as help the children outside of our state gain an appreciation for Mississippi."

-Marcus L. Thompson, Chief Administrative Officer at the Mississippi Institutions of Higher Learning

Dedicated to:

GOD, McKennley and my family:

GOD, thank you for the vision.

"The Lord answered me: Write down this vision; clearly inscribe it on tablets so one may easily read it." Habakkuk 2:2

McKennley: Without your love for reading, I would have never tried to pen a children's book. You were my inspiration. Thank you for letting me use you as my main character.

Tonya R. King and Dinah R. Wilson: Thank you for the edits. Bless you for letting your children be my children.

Peggie T. Rankin: Thank you for saying, "Publish it".

Elisha Spencer: Thank you for bringing my characters to life through your talented hands.

Love,
Tee Tee Tina
Katina Rankin

Chapter 1

McKennley Wilson is a third grader who lives up north in Harlem, New York. He is your typical nine-year-old. He plays video games all the time. He enjoys adventures. But most of all, McKennley loves to visit his favorite cousin, Ryan. Ryan lives down south in Mississippi with his two brothers, Montez and Tyler. McKennley's family was going to visit Ryan's family this summer. McKennley was so excited about his upcoming trip. Every day he asked his mother, "Are we leaving today, Mom?"

"Not yet, McKennley! We will leave in a few days," his mother Nan always answered.

"A few days. How many is a few? Is it three? Is it four? Is it five?" McKennley rattled off. He held up his right hand. He stuck one finger up and said, "One day has passed already." He raised his middle finger. "Two days have passed. When, Mom? When?"

"Soon, McKennley! Soon!" his mom answered.

McKennley ran up the stairs to his sister's room. "Kendall, what are you doing?"

" I'm packing my clothes for Mississippi, McKennley," Kendall said. " I can't wait to see Ryan, Montez, and Tyler."

"Me either! Ryan said we were going fishing," McKennley said.

"Montez told me we could jump on the trampoline," Kendall chimed in.

"We are going to have so much fun."

McKennley began jumping up and down on Kendall's bed. "I'm taking all of my video games. Woo-hoo! We're going to have fun in the country."

"What's the country, McKennley?" Kendall asked.

"You know. It's that part of the world where people talk funny. They say ' y'all '. They wear suspenders like Paul Bunyan, and they play with pigs and goats," McKennley told Kendall.

"They play with pigs and goats?" Kendall exclaimed.

"Yeah," McKennley said as he plopped down on the side of Kendall's princess bed. "Mommy says Ryan and Tyler have a farm with pigs, goats, cows, and horses. Ryan told me that he even has a pet pig named Bunky."

Princess
K

“A pet pig! You mean they don’t have cats and dogs and hamsters like us?” Kendall asked.

“That’s right. They don’t know about modern animals. You know, Kendall, I think they act like cavemen too.”

“Cavemen! What’s a caveman?” Kendall asked.

“Ah, Kendall! Don’t you first graders know anything? You know cavemen. Cavemen are the men who don’t wear shirts and who have a lot of hair all over their bodies. They carry that big stick, a club around with them everywhere,” McKennley answered.

Kendall stopped dead in her tracks. She stopped packing her Barbie dolls, turned around with her eyes stretched really, really wide and said, “Do they live in caves, McKennley?”

“You betcha! We’re going on the best adventure ever!” McKennley said as he ran out of Kendall’s room.

Chapter 2

Kendall walked over to her art set and pulled out her sketchpad. She drew a white, fluffy cat with green eyes. She also drew a puppy, a cocker spaniel, and colored it black. Proud of her artwork, she ran down the stairs into the kitchen. " Mommy, look! I drew a cat and a dog."

"Nice artwork, Kendall," Mom said.

"I am going to take these pictures to Ryan and Tyler since they don't know what modern animals look like," Kendall told her mother.

"What gives you that idea, Kendall?" her mom asked.

"McKennley told me so. He said country folk only have animals like pigs and cows. McKennley said they live in caves," Kendall continued.

Kendall's mom laughed. "Your brother has quite the imagination Kendall. Your cousins live in a house just like us, and they have dogs. Some dogs live inside like your puppy, Ivory. Some of their dogs live outside in dog houses."

"Really?" Kendall asked.

"Really," her mom said.

Kendall shot up the stairs yelling, "MCKENNLEY, MCKENNLEY! YOU TOLD ME A FIB. RYAN AND TYLER HAVE DOGS, AND THEY DON'T LIVE IN CAVES. MOM TOLD ME SO."

"Oh, Kendall! She just doesn't want to scare you, you little first grader. Trust me. You will see," McKennley vowed.

"I DON'T BELIEVE YOU," Kendall shouted.

"Well, let's just call Ryan and Tyler and ask them," McKennley said.

Ring. Ring. Ring. Ring.

"Hello."

"Hi, Cousin Pam. It's McKennley. May I speak to Ryan?"

"Sure, McKennley. How are you?" Pam asked.

"I'm fine, thank you!" McKennley answered.

"What grade are you in now?" Pam asked him.

"I'm in third grade, but I'm almost a fourth grader. I guess you could say I'm a 'third and three-quarterer', if that's a word," McKennley chuckled. "Is Ryan home?"

"RYAN!" Cousin Pam yelled.

"Yeah Ma!" Ryan answered.

"Get the phone," Pam said.

"Hello!" Ryan said.

"Hi Ryan. It's Mack and Kendall."

"Howdy, McKennley! Whatcha doing?"

"Oh, nothing! Just sitting in my room," McKennley answered. "What are you doing?"

"I'm cleaning the rooster," Ryan answered.

"Cleaning the rooster?" McKennley laughed.

"Yeah!" Ryan answered.

"Are you plucking his feathers?" McKennley asked.

"Naw, I'm just wiping them clean," Ryan said.

"You mean you have a chicken in your house?" Kendall asked in amazement.

"Yep," Ryan said. "We have a lot of roosters and hens. Some are yella, and some are black and brown."

"I told you Kendall. I told you. We are city folk. They are country folk," McKennley said pointing his finger at Kendall and laughing.

"See you in a few days, Ryan," McKennley said before hanging up.

Chapter 3

"Ma, what's a 'city folk'?" Ryan asked.

"What do you mean, Ryan?" Pam asked.

"McKennley told Kendall that they are city folk, and we are country folk," Ryan told Pam.

"Oh, Ryan! City and country just refer to the part of the United States you live in," Pam explained. "Run and get the map in your room."

Ryan sprinted to his room. He flipped on the light switch and walked over to his toy chest. He threw his G.I. Joe action figure to the right of the chest. He tossed his remote control jeep onto the floor. At the bottom of the chest, he spotted the map. Ryan grabbed the map and ran back into the living room.

"Here it is, Ma!" Ryan said enthusiastically.

Pointing to the top of the map, Pam said, "You see this state, Ryan? This is New York. It is considered a northern state. This is New York City. New York City is referred to as 'The Big Apple'! That's where McKennley lives."

"Yeah, yeah. It's also where the Statue of Liberty lives," Ryan said. "We studied that in geography."

"That's right, Ryan!" Pam said smiling. "People who live in northern states are considered 'city folk'. That's why McKennley said city folk. Now look right here. Do you know what that state is?"

"Yep," Ryan answered. "That's M-I-CROOKED LETTER-CROOKED LETTER-I-CROOKED LETTER-CROOKED LETTER-I-HUMPBACK-HUMPBACK-I," Ryan laughed. "It's Mississippi where we live."

"Good, Ryan! Mississippi is in the southern part of the country. It is considered a southern state, a more rural and country part of the United States," Pam explained.

" I get it. So, we are country folk and McKennley and Kendall are city folk," Ryan said.

"I think you have it. Are you excited about your visitors, Ryan?" Pam asked.

"So excited, Ma, sometimes I think I might wet my pants," Ryan giggled.

Ryan grabbed the map and went into his brother, Tyler's room. "What's up, Big Country?" Ryan asked.

"WHO ARE YOU CALLING COUNTRY?" Tyler screamed.

"You! Me! We're country folk. McKennley and Kendall are city folk. McKennley told me so, and see Ma showed me a map," Ryan said.

"Well, we might be country, but at least we know about nature," Tyler declared. "At least we know what ants look like. We can go into our backyard with a magnifying glass and learn how ants gather food all summer long for the winter. At least we have room to run around and play. City folk don't know about that. They don't even know what trees look like. All they have are big ole, tall buildings everywhere. Plus, they don't know anything about hunting and fishing. The only thing they know about fish is what they learned from watching 'Finding Nemo' and 'Finding Dory'! They think all fish live in a fish tank. They even wear the same clothes to school every day. They're whack, and I'm not country. Now get out of my room."

Scratching his head, Ryan turned slowly and walked out of the room. He went back into the living room and told his mother, "Ma, Tyler says city folk don't have backyards and swing sets. He said they don't even have ponds. He also said that they wear the same clothes, blue pants and white shirts, to school each day," Ryan said puzzled.

"Nonsense Ryan. You kids!" Pam said. "Now go wash up and get ready for supper."

Chapter 4

"MCKENNLEY," his mom yelled. "LET'S GO!"

"In a minute. I'm looking for my Spider-Man web blaster. Ryan says G.I. Joe is stronger than Spider-Man. I told Ryan that G.I. Joe may be stronger, but Spider-Man is wiser and can outwit G.I. Joe. We are going to let our superheroes battle it out," McKennley said.

"IF YOU ARE NOT DOWNSTAIRS IN TWO MINUTES, WE ARE GOING TO LEAVE YOU WITH THE DOG SITTER," his mom growled.

McKennley grabbed his web blaster and closed the closet door. "Got it! Coming Mother!"

"Grab your backpack, Kendall!" Mom said. "McKennley, please hurry! We need to make our flight."

Cars, trucks, and taxis were zooming by and pulling up to the curb. In and out, the vehicles came and went. The traffic guard was directing traffic with his white, gloved hand.

Soon McKennley and Kendall were on the plane with their mom. "Fasten your seatbelt," the flight attendant said as she passed the children some peanuts and juice.

"Thank you!" McKennley said as he took his drink. "My dad flies airplanes."

"He does?" the attendant replied.

"He's in the military. He flies military planes. That's why he is not with us. He had to work," McKennley told her.

Turning toward the window, McKennley pointed out the window and said, "Look Kendall, that cloud looks like a cat."

"Ooh!" Kendall sighed. "Look over there, McKennley. You can see the sun coming through that cloud. That cloud looks like a chair. Boy, I wish I could sit in it."

"Kendall, you can't sit on a cloud. You would fall right through it. Clouds are made of water. Don't you first graders know anything?"

"Know-it-all!" Kendall said as she sat back in her seat, let down her food tray and began flipping through her princess coloring book. After finding the princess she wanted to color, she asked her mom, "Should I color her apricot or caramel?"

"It's your choice, Kendall," her mom said.

“LOOK, LOOK! IT LOOKS LIKE OUR MONOPOLY BOARD, KENDALL. LOOK AT THOSE TINY HOUSES, CARS, AND TREES! THAT’S SO COOL,” McKennley shouted.

“Shhh! McKennley! Not so loud, son. Those are real houses. They will get larger as we get closer to the ground. We’re about to land. Sit back,” their mom explained to them.

“That’s the coolest thing ever, a giant monopoly board!” McKennley said under his breath. “See you later!” McKennley told the flight attendant as she walked by.

The family walked down the long hallway, rode the escalator down to the baggage terminal, and grabbed their bags. McKennley and Kendall ran to the automatic doors.

“McKennley and Kendall stop running and move away from the door,” Mom said, squinting her eyes and making an angry face.

“Aw Mom, but it is fun to feel the air blow on your face when the doors open,” Kendall said.

"Ryan!" McKennley shouted as he ran towards his cousin. "What you doing?"

"Howdy, McKennley, did you bring it?" Ryan asked him.

"Does lava shoot out of a volcano? Does a spider weave webs?" McKennley asked as he pulled his Spider-Man web blaster out of his backpack and began spraying white web strings all over Ryan.

"Kids, calm down. Get in the truck," Pam said.

On the drive to Cousin Pam's house, McKennley and Kendall saw animals grazing in a pasture.

"Look, Mom, there's a cow and a horse," Kendall exclaimed. "And that horse is gray."

"That's what we call a mule, Kendall," Ryan said.

"A mule!" Kendall asked in amazement.

"Yeah, mules help us pull the plows in the fields. Then, we go behind them and plant all sorts of food like corn, peas, and butterbeans," Ryan explained.

"Pew-ew," McKennley said. "I hate vegetables."

"A lot of people like vegetables, McKennley. That is how we make our money," Pam said.

"Make money?" McKennley asked.

"Sure. We plant and harvest our crops. We sell the vegetables to the supermarkets up north where you live. Your mom goes to the grocery store and buys the vegetables. Then, you eat them," Pam said.

"You mean they actually pay you money?" Kendall asked.

"That's right!" Pam said.

"I get money from helping Ma and Pa in the field. How do you think I buy my action hero toys?" Ryan said.

"Yeah," McKennley said. "And in those big, tall buildings in New York, folks make those action hero toys and send them down south for you to buy."

Chapter 5

They pulled up to a yellow house with green shutters.

"Okay, little people, we are here!" Mom said.

"WHERE'S THE CAVE?" Kendall yelled.

"It's around back," Ryan said.

Running full steam ahead, the kids shot around the corner of the yellow house. "What is that?" McKennley asked, pointing to a board that hung at the end of a rope.

"A tree swing," Ryan exclaimed.

McKennley said, "I have never seen one of those before. Neat!"

Right beside the swing was a trampoline. Montez and Tyler were jumping so high, Kendall thought they were going to touch the sky.

"COME ON!" Montez and Tyler screamed.

Kendall, McKennley, and Ryan ran to the trampoline and joined them.

"YIPPIE! YEAH!" The children yelled as they held hands and jumped higher and higher. When they were out of breath, they all fell down and bounced on their bottoms, laughing uncontrollably.

A blue car drove up. McKennley and Kendall's Aunt Tonya from Memphis, Tennessee, made a surprise visit home to Mississippi.

Tonya got out of the car and said, "Hello little people."

McKennley and Kendall sprinted towards her yelling, "Tee Tee Tonya!"

Their cousins, Lauren and Olivia, got out of the blue car. They all shrieked and hugged each other with very big smiles.

Kendall grabbed Olivia's right hand and said, "Come on Olivia and Lauren! Let's go and get on the trampoline."

Tee Tee Tonya said, "Wait Dear! They're too small to get on the trampoline. We're going to take their guinea pig, Tater, inside."

Tee Tee Nan said, “Yes, I’ve got their favorite squirrel book about making friends I am going to read to them.”

Lauren and Olivia’s eyes lit up. Each girl grabbed one of Tee Tee Nan’s hands, and they walked inside.

“Okay!” Kendall and McKennley said at the same time. They ran back over to the trampoline and sat down in the center of the big, black circle net.

As Kendall and McKennley observed their surroundings, they looked down a dirt pathway. Beyond the tall pine trees was the biggest cave they had ever seen.

Large, gray, cement bricks were stacked on top of each other. "It sort of looks like an igloo, but it's bigger," McKennley said.

"It's kind of scary ," Kendall added.

The boys raced down the dirt pathway with Kendall right behind them. Inside were giant bean bags and sleeping bags.

"Wow," Kendall said as she walked through the cave. "Do you guys live in here?"

"Of course not, silly," Montez said. "Mom let's us camp out here sometimes though."

Kendall kept walking through the cave. In a corner of the cave sat one, two, three, four, five, six roosters and three hens. "LOOK MCKENNLEY, CHICKENS. HERE ARE THEIR CHICKENS."

"Yep," Tyler said. "We collect them in all colors. We have a red one, a yellow one, a black one and a white one."

"Want to touch them?" Montez asked.

"Um, no!" Kendall said, jumping back. "I don't want them to peck me."

"Peck you?" Montez said while laughing. "What are you talking about Girlie? Some are stuffed like your baby dolls. Others are made of ceramic. They aren't real. They are fake."

"Fake?" Kendall said looking surprised.

McKennley and Ryan were laughing and rolling all over the floor of the cave.

"Yeah, fake," Tyler said.

"But....but," Kendall said as she gathered her thoughts. "But, Ryan said he was cleaning his chickens, and they lived in his house. He said so. He said so on the telephone."

McKennley and Ryan were laughing so hard, they were now crying.

"Gotcha, first grader," McKennley managed to squeak out while holding his stomach.

Montez grabbed Kendall's hand and said, "Come on, Kendall. Let's go to the big house and get something to drink. Those boys! Don't worry about them. We'll get them back next summer when it's time for us to go to your house up north. We'll show them! Plus, everyone knows, there is no difference between city folk and country folk."

THE END

eft top: Lauren; Left bottom: Olivia; Centered: Katina; Right top: McKennley; Right bottom: Kendall.

Katina Rankin is an Emmy-nominated television news anchor.

Katina is a native of Magee, Mississippi. She received her Bachelor's degree in Mass Communications from Alcorn State University and her Master's degree in Broadcast Journalism from Jackson State University.

She is a member of Alpha Kappa Alpha Sorority Inc., the National Academy of Television Arts and Sciences, and the National Association of Black Journalists.

She has been recognized for her reporting by the Associated Press, multiple times. Rankin is the recipient of the Martin Luther King, Jr. Community Service Award, the Athletes for Progress Award and has been honored by many other prestigious organizations. Rankin has also been named Mississippi's Woman of the Year.

Made in the USA
Columbia, SC
04 July 2017